Lake Michigan Beach Days

By Russell Slater
Illustrated by Tanya Glebova

ISBN-13:
978-1724878359

ISBN-10:
1724878352

Peninsulam Publishing

Stories Made in Michigan

www.peninsulampublishing.com

Printed in the USA

For:

Eli (a sand lover)
Mom (a beach lover)
and
Lula (a pretty book for you)

Hi there! My name is Sandy, and I love going to the beach! I'm what some would call a "beach bum." I can't get enough water and sunshine! It puts me in a good mood and always makes me happy. Lake Michigan is my favorite lake to visit. Its beaches are amazing!

Lake Michigan is one of five Great Lakes, and it has over 1,400 miles of shoreline. We live in the heart of the largest group of freshwater lakes in the entire world! As a Michigander, you are never more than 6 miles from the water, be it one of our Great Lakes, or one of the thousands of smaller lakes, rivers, streams, or ponds in the state.

At the beginning of summer, I made it my goal to visit some of the best beaches along Lake Michigan. Come with me as I find all sorts of ways to enjoy life along the water!

*The name "Michigan" is believed to come from "Michi-gami," the Ojibwe term meaning "Great Water."

Watching the boats at Silver Lake is so relaxing!

With Lake Michigan on one side and Silver Lake on the other, the Silver Lake State Park has more than 2,000 acres of dunes for me to enjoy! Sometimes there's nothing I like more than watching the boats going to and from the beach along the 3-mile long park, which also has access to a mile of Silver Lake's beach.

*The nearly 3,000-acre Silver Lake State Park is near Mears, Michigan, and includes the Little Sable Point Lighthouse.

Building sandcastles is so much fun!

I have a blast building magnificent castles fit for a queen on South Haven's South Beach! And the view of the big red lighthouse can't be beat! Although it can get a little crowded during the summer months, the beach on the south side of where the Black River meets Lake Michigan is one of my favorites.

*Almost all of the city of South Haven is within Van Buren County, but part of it stretches into neighboring Allegan County to the north.

Ice cream? Yes, please! One of my favorite ways
to cool off on a hot day is with a creamy cone in hand,
especially on the gorgeous Oval Beach in Saugatuck.
Surrounded by powdery sand dunes, Oval Beach is
known throughout the country as one of the best
places for hours of fun under the sun.

Enjoy a cold treat!

*The Kalamazoo River divides
the city of Saugatuck in half before
linking up to Lake Michigan.

Let's go surfing!

With its one-of-a-kind tunnel through a sand dune, Holland's 22-acre Tunnel Park is a fantastic choice for spending quality time with friends and family. When I'm not riding waves, I love playing on the playground, climbing the dune stairway, or playing volleyball.

*Holland is home to a significant population of Dutch-descended residents, a fact celebrated every May when the city hosts the Tulip Time Festival.

I love to kick up my feet and bury my face in a good book!

If I need a break between chapters, I like to gaze upon Grand Haven's lighthouse and pier. When beachgoers like me seek a good time, we head to the beach at the 48-acre Grand Haven State Park.

*Grand Haven State Park is east of Lake Michigan, and South of the Grand River.

Go fly a kite!

*Silver Beach Park is located near the
mouth of the St. Joseph River.

Silver Beach, tucked beneath a steep bluff in the city of St. Joseph, stretches for 1,600 feet – plenty of room for local residents and visitors like me to fly a kite or have other fun.

I also really enjoy exploring the South Pier when I'm not kite flying or swimming.

Have a picnic on the beach!

One of my favorite places to sit and eat is the beach at the Pere Marquette Park in Muskegon! With the Muskegon Channel to the north, I can choose any spot to spread out along the 2.5 miles of beachfront. If I want even more water fun, Muskegon Lake is just a short walk away!

*Muskegon has the largest population of any city along Lake Michigan's east coast.

Walk your dog!

When I want to take my dog for a stroll, fish from the pier, or just observe the local wildlife, the Manistique Boardwalk is the place to go! Extending 1.83 miles from the edge of the city of Manistique, the boardwalk and its Upper Peninsula view of Lake Michigan is one of the best!

*Manistique is near Kitch-Iti-Kipi, Michigan's largest spring.

Rock skipping in Ludington!

It's fun to see the rocks skip along the water – whether on Lake Michigan or Hamlin Lake – at the 5,300-acre Ludington State Park! Located at the mouth of the Pere Marquette River, this park has dunes, woodland, a river, and a lake – it has a little bit of everything!

*Ludington is the port of origin for the S.S. Badger, a ferry boat that transports people and vehicles between Michigan and Wisconsin during the summer.

The dune tour at Sleeping Bear Dunes National Lakeshore is my favorite place to snap some one-of-a-kind pictures. The 35-mile beach is near Empire, Michigan, and is a part of the national park which also includes North and South Manitou islands.

Ride your buggy at
the Sleeping Bear Dunes!

*In some places, the Sleeping Bear Dunes
reach over 450 feet above Lake Michigan.

Go hunting for Petoskey stones!

I love to find the Michigan state stone, the Petoskey Stone, along the beach at the Petoskey State Park. 3 miles to the north of Petoskey, the park's beach is along the Little Traverse Bay.

*Petoskey Stones are found primarily in the northwestern section of Michigan's Lower Peninsula, but some have also been discovered on the northeastern side of the "Mitten."

It's part surfing, part sailing – let's go windsurfing!

The white sands of Charlevoix's Lake Michigan Beach are at fantastic place to catch some waves - or just lay in the sun! I like to dry off while taking a leisurely walk on the South Pier, or dropping a fishing line into the water below.

*The city of Charlevoix is surrounded by water, particularly Lake Charlevoix, Lake Michigan, and Round Lake.

Ride a watercraft in Traverse City!

Year after year, I always come back to Clinch Park in Traverse City! The 1,500-foot park beach is on the shore of Grand Traverse Bay, a Lake Michigan bay created by the Leelanau Peninsula.

*The Traverse City region is known for being the largest producer of cherries in the country, a fact locals celebrate during the annual Cherry Festival.

SEE YOU !

TO EACH THEIR BEACH!

So get out there. Take a deep breath of fresh air.
Listen to the waves. Explore, play, laugh, and enjoy all
that Lake Michigan's beautiful beaches have to offer.

Stick your toes in the sand, feel the sunshine on your
face, and the breeze in your hair.

Soak it in.

ABOUT THE AUTHOR

Russell Slater is an author from western Michigan. He has written sixteen books, and his work has been published in the (Wayland) *Penasee Globe*, *Allegan County News*, *Engraver's Journal*, *Flavor 616 Magazine*, and *the Volunteer: Civil Air Patrol Magazine*.

He lives in a rural community with his wife and son.

Contact the author:

Russell@peninsulampublishing.com

ABOUT THE ILLUSTRATOR

Tanya Glebova loves drawing pictures and illustrating books. She specializes in character design and realism.

She currently lives in Kharkov, Ukraine, where she recently graduated from the post-graduate program in fine arts.

"There is no greater reward for me than to have my drawings make people smile."

Don't miss these other
entertaining, educational
children's books from

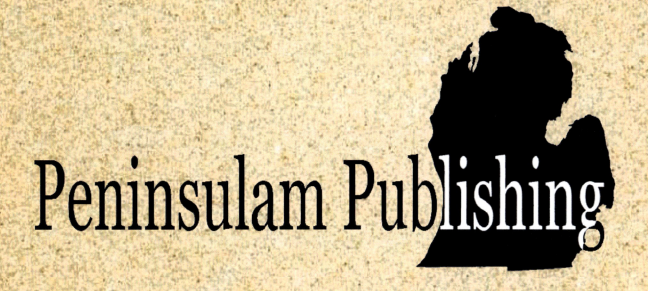

Peninsulam Publishing

Publishing stories Made in Michigan

All books available at www.peninsulampublishing.com

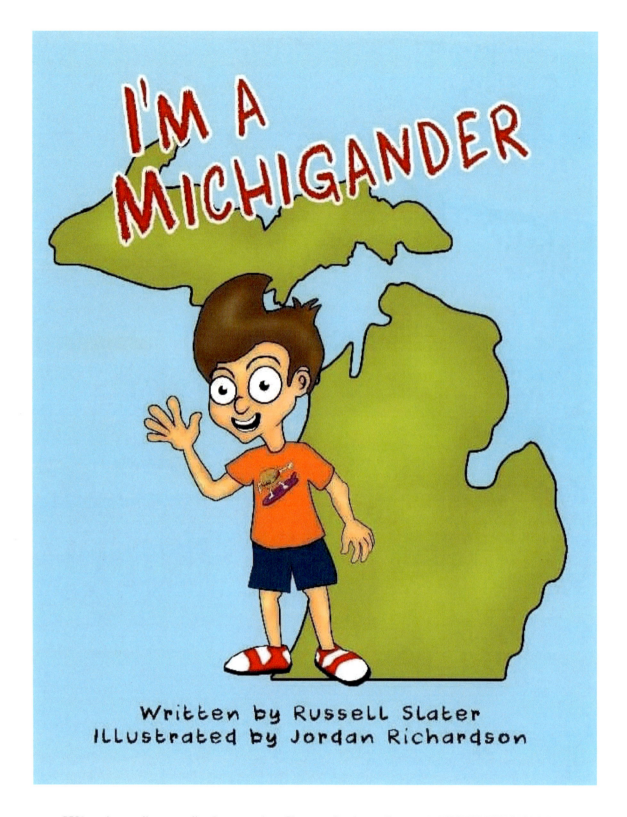

What's so "great" about the Great Lakes State? EVERYTHING!!!

From lake to glistening lake, this precious pair of peninsulas holds a special place in the hearts of those lucky enough to call Michigan "home."

Join us on a journey across the state and learn why we're proud to say, "I'M A MICHIGANDER!"

US $12.99

EDDY ELK AND MANDY MOOSE

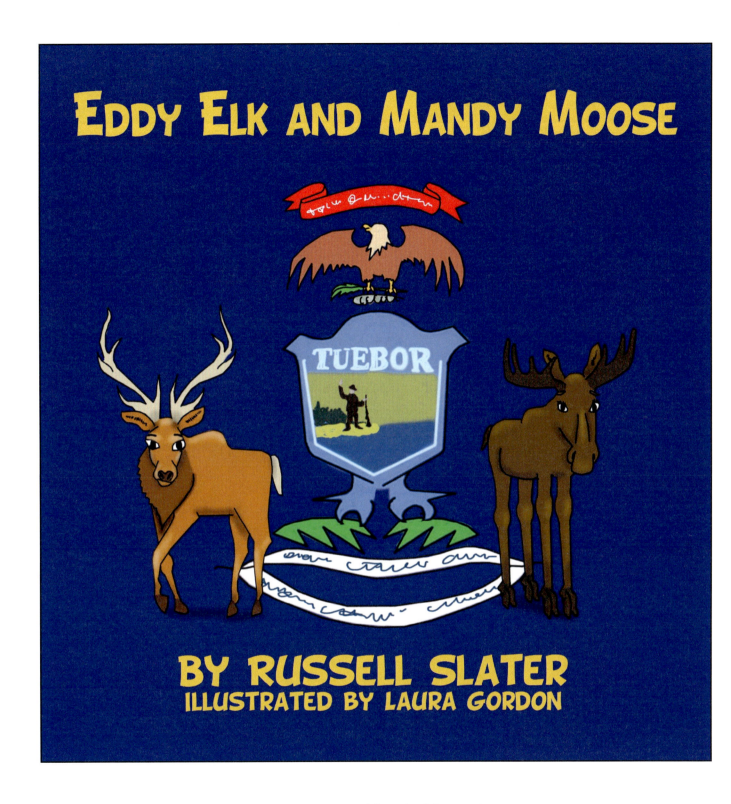

BY RUSSELL SLATER
ILLUSTRATED BY LAURA GORDON

Eddy Elk and Mandy Moose have
stepped out of the flag, they're on the loose!

Join the adventurous pair as they explore the natural wonders of the Great
Lakes State. From the Petoskey stone to the Whitetail deer, learn why there is
no place on Earth quite like Michigan.

U.S. $9.99

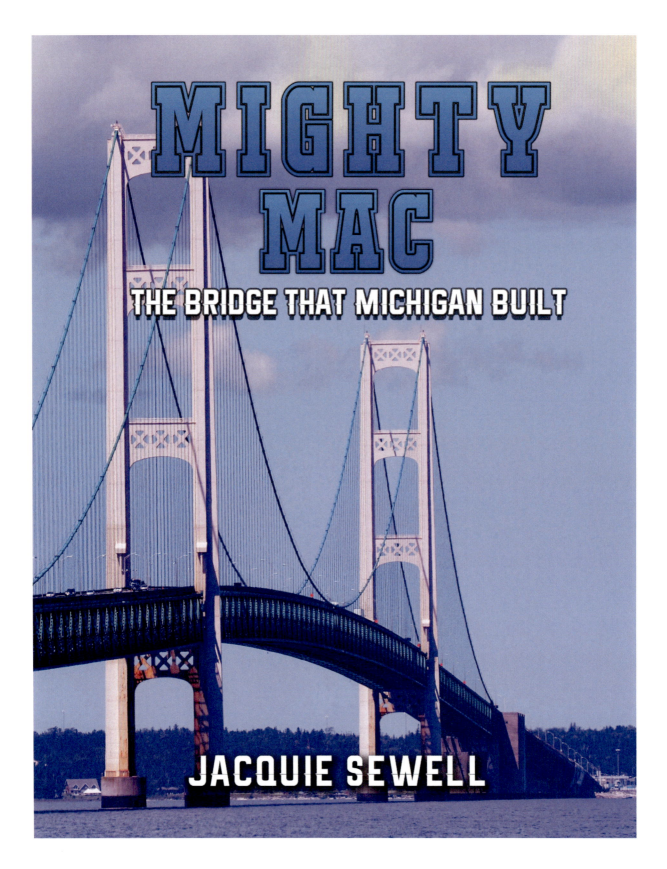

MIGHTY MAC

THE BRIDGE THAT MICHIGAN BUILT

JACQUIE SEWELL

A plan once thought impossible, men and resources came together to realize the dream of uniting the Upper and Lower Peninsulas of Michigan. Explore the creation of Michigan's shining achievement, the construction of the Mackinac Bridge, in *Mighty Mac, The Bridge That Michigan Built.*

US $12.99

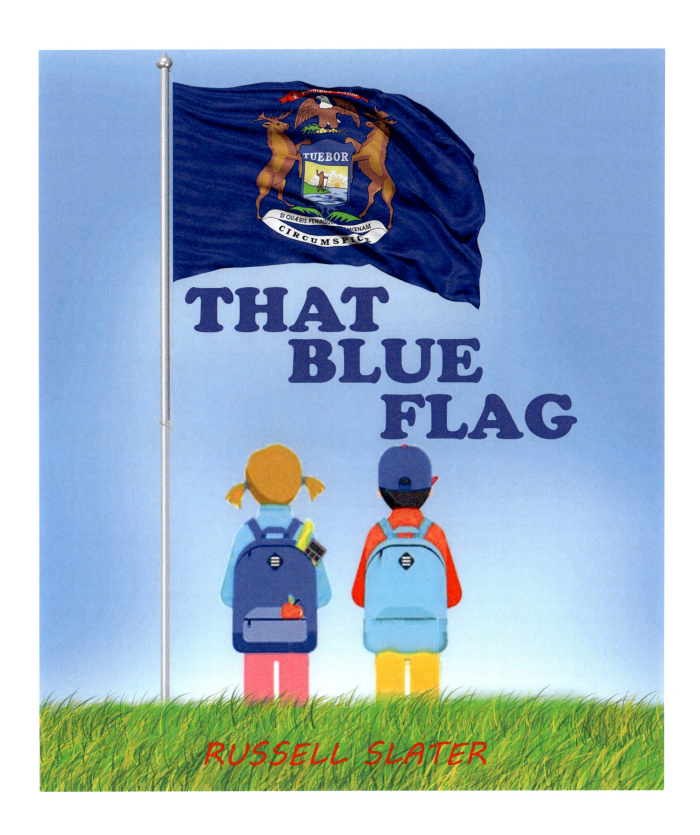

THAT BLUE FLAG

RUSSELL SLATER

"What's that blue flag?

Why, that's our Michigan flag, and it's full of meaning! Step into my classroom and let me tell you all about it..."

US $9.99

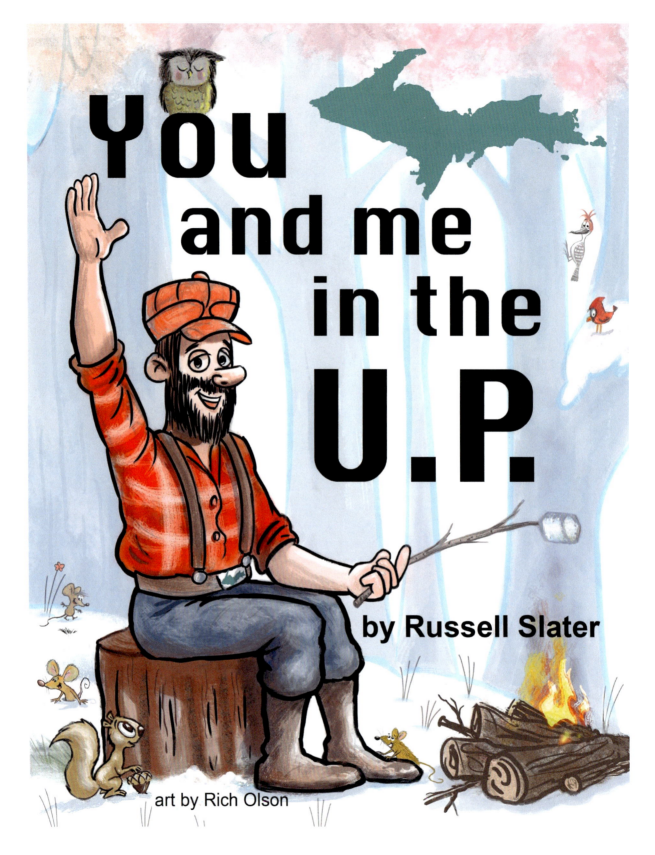

You and me in the U.P.

by Russell Slater

art by Rich Olson

Take a peek at the pleasant peninsula treasured by Michiganders both north
and south of the Mackinac Bridge.
From the Pictured Rocks, to the Soo Locks...
The U.P. awaits you and me.

Michigan's Upper Peninsula: It's like a whole other state!
U.S. $9.99

Michigan Author Russell Slater
LOVES to visit schools!

Interested in an author visit?
For flexible rates and availability, email
Russell@peninsulampublishing.com

Made in the USA
Lexington, KY
09 September 2018